COIN FINDS IN BRITAIN
A COLLECTOR'S GUIDE

Michael Cuddeford

SHIRE PUBLICATIONS

SHIRE PUBLICATIONS
Bloomsbury Publishing Plc

Kemp House, Chawley Park, Oxford OX2 9PH, UK
29 Earlsfort Terrace, Dublin 2, Ireland
1385 Broadway, 5th Floor, New York, NY 10018, USA
Email: shire@bloomsbury.com
www.shirebooks.co.uk

SHIRE is a trademark of Osprey Publishing Ltd

First published in Great Britain in 2013

A CIP catalogue record for this book is available from the
British Library.

Shire Library no. 746
Print ISBN: 978 0 74781 244 9
ePub: 978 0 74781 346 0
ePDF: 978 0 74781 349 1

Michael Cuddeford has asserted his right under the
Copyright, Designs and Patents Act, 1988, to be identified
as the author of this book.

Designed by Tony Truscott Designs, Sussex, UK
Typeset in Perpetua and Gill Sans.
Printed and bound in India by Replika Press Private Ltd.

22 23 24 25 26   15 14 13 12 11 10

The Woodland Trust
Shire Publications supports the Woodland Trust, the UK's
leading woodland conservation charity.

www.shirebooks.co.uk
To find out more about our authors and books visit our
website. Here you will find extracts, author interviews,
details of forthcoming events and the option to sign-up
for our newsletter.

COVER IMAGE
A selection of coins from various periods.

TITLE PAGE IMAGE
The obverse of a silver groat of Edward III.

CONTENTS PAGE IMAGE
The reverse of an Iron Age gold stater.

EDITOR'S NOTE
Please note that coins are not all shown to the same scale.

ACKNOWLEDGEMENTS
I am most grateful to the following who provided items for
photography, gave helpful advice, or permitted access to
land for research purposes: Roger Barrett, Roy Boreham,
Andrew Cook, Elizabeth Cottam, Keith Cullum,
Alfred Daines, Joseph Fay, Anthony Holmes, Roger and
Keith Knight, Donald McGowan, Clive Matthews, Martin
Matthews, Peter Matthews, Richard Matthews, Alexander
Micklem, Andrew Palmer, Grant Peakall, David Powell,
Chris Rudd, Clive, Mark and Ruth Stephens, Philip
Skingsley, David Stacey, Robert Thomas, Mike Vosper,
Alistair Wardle, Martin and Tina Warder.

Illustrations are acknowledged as follows (numbered
according to their position left to right, row by row down
a page): Chris Rudd, page 14 (6 & 9), page 15 (4, 6 & 10),
page 16 (4, 9 & 10), page 17 (1, 2, 5, 8 & 9). Mike Vosper,
page 14 (3 & 4), page 15 (1, 3, & 9), page 16 (1,2, & 5),
page 17 (6 & 10), page 34 (1 & 8), page 35 (2).
Spink & Son, page 49 (2).

CONTENTS

BRITAIN'S BURIED COINAGE

COINS HAVE BEEN used in Britain for over two thousand years, and throughout that period have been lost, discarded or deliberately buried. Over the centuries, successive generations have found such coins from earlier times in the course of farming or building activities, and since the nineteenth century have actively sought them through archaeology and, more recently, metal detecting. This book is intended to act as a guide to the range of coins to be found buried in the soil of Britain, and to categorise them broadly according to type and historical period. The thing that probably surprises people the most is the sheer volume of early coins that have found their way into the buried historic landscape. On some Roman sites coin finds may number in the hundreds or even thousands, and even in landscapes of no obvious historic importance early coins may still be surprisingly prolific. So how do coins come to be buried in the first place?

Deliberate concealment is of course one way, and over the years the media have carried stories of some quite spectacular finds, such as the Hoxne

Opposite:
A range of coins dating from the late Iron Age to modern times, all typical of single finds from farmland.

Left: A hoard of Roman gold *solidi*, dating from the late fourth to early fifth century AD. Found in Essex (average diameter 21 mm).

5

Not all hoards are large and spectacular – these three early Saxon pennies (late seventh to early eighth century AD) were found in close proximity, but loose in ploughsoil. They were subsequently declared Treasure (actual size 12mm).

Roman treasure. Other hoards may contain only a handful of coins, but still represent a deliberate attempt by someone to conceal portable wealth from the risk of theft by others. Sometimes hoards are associated with specific periods of civil disorder, such as wars or invasion, and in such circumstances hoards continue to be buried in troubled parts of the world. Hoards, however, are not always the result of concealment for recovery. Just as people throw coins into fountains and wells for good luck, the same superstition was prevalent in ancient times, to the extent that high-value coins and artefacts were buried as votive offerings, with no intention of recovery on the part of the owner. It is now thought that the amazing assemblage of Iron Age gold found at Snettisham in Norfolk, and now in the British Museum, was in all probability deliberately abandoned as an offering to the gods, and this has even been suggested for the Hoxne hoard. It is quite possible that many smaller coin hoards were also votive deposits, rather than concealed with the intention of later recovery.

However, most coins that are found by archaeologists or members of the public are single finds, of which the majority will be casual losses. That this happens can be seen by looking around on the ground by vending machines and parking meters, where odd coins can occasionally be spotted. Many ancient coins were a lot smaller and lighter than modern ones, and, even allowing for people taking more care of them, an amazingly large number seem to have been lost. Of course, just as some hoards were buried for votive purposes, the same is probably true of single coins, which may have been deposited at sacred sites in some quantity. If, for example, a metal-detector user recovers a number of coins with a date range spanning several centuries in an open field with no obvious archaeology evident, they might be interpreted as casual losses, but in ancient times there could have been a venerated tree or sacred grove at the very same spot, and the coins may have been deliberately placed in and around the site, even though nothing remains in the archaeological record other than the coins themselves. Similarly, a single coin may have been placed in a field or other location as a one-off act of devotion to a particular god or for general good fortune. A very high number of gold coins from the Iron Age have been found as single finds, which means that their owners must have been remarkably careless to lose so many in everyday transactions, unless they were deliberately deposited. In later periods gold coin finds are extremely rare, because they were too valuable for day-to-day transactions. When lower-value coins are found by themselves it is probable that they represent casual losses, but that is not something that we can ever say with certainty.

Where locations produce random scatters of coins covering broad periods, there will probably have been several mechanisms at work at the same time. As already stated, some Roman occupation sites can be extremely

Iron Age gold stater, dating from the first century BC to the first century AD. A single find but possibly a deliberate votive offering (actual size 20 mm).

prolific, and coins recovered from such sites will undoubtedly derive from small plough-scattered hoards, votive deposits and also casual losses. From the third century AD, Roman coins were produced in vast quantities and during some periods single coins would have been of very little intrinsic value. These were undoubtedly lost through use just as modern small change is lost, and as they were of low value, little effort would have been expended in looking for them. Some may even have been simply discarded when they were rendered worthless in one of the frequent re-coinages of the Roman period. But if we assume that some at least were lost through use, there has to be active trading going on in the first place, and many Roman period sites may have been occupied as nucleated settlements much like later medieval villages, even though the archaeological interpretation is generally to see them as self-subsisting agricultural units. If this latter was wholly the case, it is difficult to see how so many coins could have been lost, if they were not being actively exchanged.

Typical finds from a Roman period rural site (largest coin 19 mm).

That coins are lost where they are used is demonstrated by the example already cited of small change falling around vending machines, and metal-detector users who search the sites of travelling fairs will usually find a good haul of dropped coins after the fair has moved on. Those who search parkland sometimes find coins in small stacks, lying as they fell, having slipped from the trouser pocket of someone sitting on the grass. Some measure of coin circulation in the seventeenth century can be gauged from the traders' tokens that prevailed for a short period. These were issued by local tradesmen, who were normally the only persons who could redeem them for cash. Most traders' tokens that occur as field finds are local to the find-spot, with just the occasional one turning up from further away. This demonstrates that, at least in this case, loss was related to locale. However, it is highly likely that a proportion of coins found as single field finds were not originally lost there, but arrived at the location by other means. There are some fields that produce significant numbers of coins of many periods, and yet which have no history of any sort of on-site trading taking place. In ancient times coins were normally carried in purses or pouches, not loose in pockets, if indeed early garments even had pockets, and so they are unlikely to have been lost in the places they are found. The most probable mechanism for the presence of many single coin finds is that of secondary deposition, with the coins being lost elsewhere but being brought to the location in domestic refuse, which was used for manuring fields. Prior to flushing lavatories and domestic rubbish collection, the disposal of human and animal waste was an ever-present problem; the removal of such material, with that from privies being known colloquially as 'night soil', was undertaken by men employed specifically for the job. The waste was carted out from the cities and into the countryside, where it was made available to farmers for fertiliser. The rural population was probably too small for it to produce enough waste of its own to adequately manure large growing areas, and it may be that many of the coin finds from arable land originally came from an urban centre many miles away. This would certainly explain the occasional find of high-value coins, which probably saw little circulation in the rural economy. This process was probably going on way back in antiquity, and even up to the early twentieth century the amount of horse manure alone that descended daily on to the streets of Britain's cities was enormous. Any coin or other small personal item dropped into a privy or on to a manure-covered street was gone for ever, and could be destined to be re-deposited on a field many miles from the place where it was originally lost.

As well as secondary deposition, there are other considerations to be taken into account when assessing the

The reverse of an early second century AD coin. The amount of wear suggests that it may not have been lost until the last part of the third century (actual size 32 mm).

meaning of coin finds in a historical context. Whether coins arrive by primary or secondary deposition, they also move around in the soil when a location is subjected to cultivation. Ploughing itself does not move buried objects laterally to any extent, but secondary cultivation certainly does. Harrows and cultivators, particularly powered ones, can move coins and small objects considerable distances, and research has demonstrated that this can be a matter of a hundred metres or more over a

Archaeologists excavating a Roman site.

period of time. Coins might also adhere to ploughshares, and be redeposited at the opposite end of a field when a plough is re-inserted, or be carried on the mud of tractor tyres before dropping off elsewhere.

When trying to decide when a coin may have been deposited, the amount of wear on a coin might be taken as an indication. At the time of decimalisation in Britain in 1971, many worn Victorian coppers were still in circulation, some more than a hundred years old. The same applies to ancient coins, which may have circulated for even longer periods. Another factor to include is immobilisation. A coin might go into a savings deposit for many years, only to be returned to circulation, but in an unworn condition despite being the same age as very worn coins of the same date.

Whatever mechanisms were at work, the fact is that the soil of Britain contains an amazing legacy of our land's numismatic history, and the following pages are intended to give the reader a guide to the more common types of coin that are likely to be encountered.

A metal-detecting rally in progress.

IRON AGE COINS

THE TERM 'Iron Age' describes a period from roughly the eighth century BC to the first century AD, its origin being the adoption of iron as the metal of choice for tools and weapons; these had previously been made from copper-alloy, during what is known as the 'Bronze Age'. In the past historians have always explained the advent of the British Iron Age in terms of invasions by new peoples, but archaeology now favours a migration of technology rather than an incursion of population, although demographic changes may well have occurred towards the end of the period. What little we know about the peoples of Iron Age Britain derives from classical writers, but we must be aware that they probably omitted far more than they told us. During the Roman period the names of indigenous tribes were identified with geographical areas, and numismatists have ever since tried to attribute coins to these tribes, based on the areas in which specific coin types predominate. This is without doubt deeply flawed, for there is every reason to believe that there were many more tribes than those named by the Romans, and that the tribal territories may well have been quite different prior to the Roman invasions; some areas of southern Britain may even have been ruled for a time by kings based in Gaul (modern France). The peoples of Iron Age western Europe used to be labelled 'Celts' by early historians, but these days it is regarded as more realistic to simply refer to them as 'Iron Age peoples', and to describe their coins as either 'Gaulish' or 'British', depending on where they are mostly found.

The use of coinage spread to western Europe in the fourth century BC and the first coins were copies of Greek issues. We know from historical narratives that several Greek states employed western European warriors as mercenaries, and that these were paid in gold coin. Thus the first Iron Age coins copy those of Macedon, Syracuse, Tarentum and Carthage, and in western Europe the predominant prototype is a gold coin, termed a 'stater', issued in great quantity by the Macedonian ruler Philip II. These staters were copied by a number of Gaulish tribes, who applied their own distinctive artistic interpretation and produced coins of quite spectacular abstract design.

Opposite:
Detail from a
North Thames
gold quarter-stater.
First century AD
(12 mm).

The earliest coins that are found in Britain are copper-alloy issues from Carthage. These have been found in sufficient quantity to suggest that they were contemporary imports, but it is not known what monetary use they had, if any. The first coins to have widespread use were broad-flan gold staters struck in western Gaul, which may have been imported into Britain by way of trade, or with a migration of peoples, or quite possibly both. These have a very abstracted head on the obverse and a charioteer on the reverse. One very distinctive feature on these coins, and indeed of subsequent British issues, is a 'spike' above the ear plus neck ornamentation below the bust. These are not features of the Macedonian prototypes but may be found in the hair adornment and neck decoration on Syracusan and Carthaginian gold coins of the period and these, rather than the issues of Philip II, may have been the inspiration for this type of stater. Another variety of stater that has widespread distribution in Southern and Eastern Britain is a Gaulish import with a blank obverse, and a very stylised horse on the reverse. These were struck in great quantity and it is speculated that they relate to the Gallic wars of Julius Caesar, and perhaps represent a coinage struck to pay a confederation of warriors raised to resist the Romans. In addition to gold staters, quarter-staters were also struck; some copy the designs of the full staters but there was a very widespread issue in which the obverse head and reverse chariot have become abstracted to the point of being geometric patterns. We have no idea whether any of these coins represent one dominant polity ruling over a wide area, or if they were used by different tribes as a common currency. Numismatists identify the different coin types of the period by means of letters, e.g. type 'A', type 'B', and so on.

During the first century BC, British tribes began issuing coins in imitation of the Gaulish imports. These continued the process of abstraction and fall into discrete regional groupings, each with their own distinctive style. Following Caesar's conquest of Gaul and incursions into Britain, Roman silver coins became familiar to the western European tribes, and these were used as the prototypes for a wide range of silver issues. Some, possibly struck by pro-Roman rulers, copy classical imagery, whilst others were produced in very much the native style. Some polities also issued copper-alloy coins, which presumably catered for a localised market economy, although there was no overall tri-metallic system and economic circumstances must have been very changeable and localised.

Greek prototype and possible prototypes for some Iron Age gold coins. Fourth–third century BC (largest 18 mm).

A copper-alloy coin struck at Carthage, but found in Kent. Fourth–third century BC (17 mm).

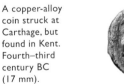

Most Iron Age coins were conventionally struck by hand between two dies, but some were cast in moulds, notably in the South-Western zone and also in the South-Eastern and North Thames regions, where they were cast in conjoined strips and then individually separated. These latter were made from a copper alloy with a high tin and lead content, which is termed 'potin' by some numismatists. This method of production was widespread in Gaul but we have no idea as to who the issuing authority was in Britain, or if the coins were fractional denominations or a separate coinage entirely. The coins are based on issues from the Greek colony of Massalia (modern Marseilles). One type has a very stylised head on the obverse, and a butting bull on the reverse. A commoner type has the same motifs, but the coins are much flatter and the imagery even more abstracted. In addition to struck coins, many plated forgeries of Iron Age coins are found. It is not known if these were deliberate attempts to deceive, or if some may have been produced with official sanction for a specific purpose.

The first Iron Age coins produced in Britain were uninscribed, but later on legends began to appear, giving the names of issuers and mint locations. Many of the names are unknown to us but a few can be identified from historical sources, allowing us for the first time to put the coins into some sort of historical and chronological order. Because of the uncertainty involved in trying to attribute coins to tribes named in ancient sources, I prefer to relate them to the regions in which they normally occur. The following table lists these regions by name, the modern counties that they incorporate, and the names of tribes thought to have occupied those areas for at least part of the coin-issuing period. Precise dating of Iron Age coins is rarely possible, but in general terms the British uninscribed issues probably date from around 150 to 40 BC, the inscribed issues from 40 BC to AD 43, in some cases possibly a little after.

North-Eastern: Lincolnshire, Leicestershire, Nottinghamshire, Humberside and possibly into South Yorkshire. Tribe: Corieltauvi, formally known as Coritani.

Eastern: Norfolk, north Cambridgeshire and north Suffolk. Tribe: Iceni.

North Thames: Essex, Hertfordshire, Bedfordshire, south Cambridgeshire, south Suffolk. Tribes: Catuvellauni and Trinovantes.

South-Eastern: Kent. Tribe: Cantii.

Southern: Berkshire, Surrey, Sussex, parts of Hampshire. Tribes: Atrebates, Regni and Belgae (Suessiones?).

South-Western: Dorset, Somerset, Wiltshire, parts of Hampshire. Tribe: Durotriges.

Western: Gloucestershire, parts of Hereford and Worcester, Somerset, Oxfordshire and Wiltshire. Tribe: Dobunni.

GOLD STATERS, SECOND TO FIRST CENTURY BC

Imported, `Type 'A', 24 mm. Corresponding quarter-staters are also found.

Imported, Type 'E', 18 mm.

North-Eastern, 18 mm.

Eastern, 'Norfolk Wolf' type, 18 mm.

North Thames, 'Clacton' type, 20 mm.

North Thames, Cunobelinos, 18 mm.

North Thames and South-Eastern, Dubnovellaunos, 19 mm. (Coins from North Thames have an obverse wreath; those from the South-Eastern region a blank obverse.)

North Thames and Southern, 'Westerham' type, 20 mm.

North Thames and Southern, 'Whaddon Chase' type, 18 mm.

GOLD STATERS, FIRST CENTURY BC TO FIRST CENTURY AD

Southern, uninscribed, 19 mm.

Southern, Verica, 19 mm.

South-Western (usually white gold or silver),
18 mm.

Western, Corio, 18 mm. (There are several
variations of this type with different names.)

GOLD QUARTER-STATERS, FIRST CENTURY BC TO FIRST CENTURY AD

Imported, North Thames and Southern,
'geometric' types, 12 mm.

Eastern, 11 mm.

North Thames and Southern, 'Qc' type, 13 mm.

North Thames, Addedomaros, 12 mm.

South-Eastern, 13 mm.

Southern, Tincomaros, 12 mm.

SILVER UNITS, FIRST CENTURY BC TO FIRST CENTURY AD

North-Eastern, 'boar/horse' type, 13 mm.

North-Eastern, 'Aun Cost', 14 mm.

Eastern, 'head/horse' type, 13 mm.

Eastern, 'boar/horse' type, 11 mm.

Eastern, 'Anted', 13 mm.

North Thames type, 10 mm.

North Thames, Cunobelinos, 14 mm.

North Thames and South-Eastern type, 13 mm.

South-Eastern, Amminios, 12 mm.

Southern, Epatticos, 12 mm.

SILVER UNITS, FIRST CENTURY BC TO FIRST CENTURY AD

South-Western type, 11 mm.

Western, 'Eisv', 12 mm.

COPPER-ALLOY UNITS, FIRST CENTURY BC TO FIRST CENTURY AD

North Thames/South-Eastern, cast, 18 mm.

North Thames/South-Eastern, cast, 18 mm.

North Thames, 14 mm.

North Thames, 'Ver', 15 mm.

North Thames, Cunobelinos, 16 mm.

South-Eastern, Dubnovellaunos, 14 mm.

Southern, 15 mm.

South-Western, cast, 16 mm.

ROMAN COINS

THE ROMAN OCCUPATION of Britain lasted nearly four centuries, from AD 43 until the early fifth century. During this time the use of coinage became widespread, and Roman coins are amongst the commonest types of artefact to be found on archaeological sites of the period. The appearance of Roman coins was not a novelty to the native Britons; coins of the Roman republic are found in Iron Age contexts, so clearly were imported and used, and the raids by Julius Caesar in the first century BC probably resulted in a further limited influx of Roman coinage.

At the time of the invasion, the Roman monetary system consisted of a gold unit, the *aureus*, a silver coin called the *denarius*, a large brass coin called a *sestertius*, a smaller brass coin called a *dupondius* and a similar-sized copper coin called an *as*. Until the third century AD, multiple coin units were distinguished by the emperor being depicted with a radiate, or spiked, crown, whilst on most other coins he was depicted with a laurel wreath. This is a further distinction between the *dupondius* and the *as*, with the former, being worth two *asses*, having a radiate bust and the latter a laureate one. There were also other fractions of these units, but they rarely occur as site finds in Britain. During the Roman period the silver content of the *denarius* became progressively debased until, in the early third century, the emperor Marcus Aurelius Antoninus, known to history as 'Caracalla', introduced a new silver multiple unit, possibly tariffed at two *denarii*. As multiples, these have a radiate rather than laureate bust, and are sometimes referred to as '*antoniniani*' by coin collectors, named after the emperor who introduced them. Already baser than the *denarii* they replaced, the new radiate unit itself was rapidly debased and within a few decades was predominantly a copper-alloy coin with just a small silver content, evident only as a silver surface deposit that only rarely survives on excavated coins.

In AD 258 the provinces of Britain, together with Gaul and Germany, formed a breakaway enclave under a succession of rulers until AD 273, when the empire was reunited. Copper-alloy radiates of these rulers are quite common as site finds, as are coins of the central empire, which were presumably still entering Britain. Also around AD 273 the emperor Aurelian reformed the coinage with the introduction of a re-tariffed radiate and a copper-alloy laureate issue. Both are comparatively scarce as site finds. A further reform was carried out by Diocletian in *c.* AD 286, when a new silver coin was introduced, followed by a new and large copper-alloy laureate coin some years later. Although these copper-alloy coins occur as British site finds, the silver issues do not, other than some rare issues of the emperor Carausius. Carausius was a military commander who, in AD 287, formed another breakaway kingdom out of Britain and part of Gaul. He issued radiates in accordance with central government coins and a silver coin that presumably corresponded to those of Diocletian.

The next major change to the Roman monetary system occurred during the reign of Constantine the Great. The gold *aureus* was replaced by a new coin called the *solidus*. Two new silver coins were introduced, for which we do not know the ancient names, but which are popularly referred to as the '*miliarense*' and the '*siliqua*'. The former rarely occur as single finds but the latter are quite common. The copper-alloy coinage was reformed and a number of reverse types were produced that were shared by co-emperors and regents, and so from this time on it is the reverse type rather than the ruler by which Roman coins are generally listed. A further revision of the coinage was undertaken in AD 348, with the introduction of new and much larger copper-alloy coins, which rapidly became reduced in size. The revolt of Magnentius in AD 350 brought with it the usurper's own attempt to reform the copper-alloy issues. Another reform occurred in AD 364 when yet another new copper-alloy series was introduced, and finally, in AD 378, a further new issue of small copper-alloy coins was struck, which were to be the last coins used in Roman Britain. As numismatists do not know the contemporary names of any of these coins, it has become the convention to refer to them as *nummi*, the word *nummus* simply being Latin for 'coin'.

Throughout the Roman period the forgery of imperial coins was a continuous problem. The earliest copies are those of Claudius, dating to the invasion period, and it may be that these were struck by quasi-official mints under the aegis of the army, perhaps because the troops were being too remote from the imperial supply lines that would normally have delivered military pay. During its period of issue, the silver *denarius* was subjected to extensive copying, with base silver or silver-plated coins being commonplace. By the mid-third century the small base radiates had driven the larger denominations out of existence and, increasingly, irregular copies of these also were being struck, with increasing degrees of crudeness and reduction in size. Some are less than 10 millimetres in diameter. These are known colloquially as 'barbarous radiates', and are very common site finds in Britain. Other 'epidemics' of copying targeted the *nummi* of AD 330–48 and the reformed issues of 348–50. Of the latter, the 'fallen horseman' reverse is the most widely imitated, and probably more than half of all coins from this period that occur as site finds are irregular. Another phenomenon of this period was the cutting down in size of the larger official coins into small discs of 10 millimetres or less in diameter, presumably in an attempt to adjust them to a new tariff.

Gold *aureus* of Claudius (AD 41–54), struck to commemorate his conquest of Britain, 19 mm.

The use of coins in Roman Britain seems to have been very much connected with the military, which throughout the occupation was maintained at a high level in relation to the civilian population. Britain was never completely conquered, with the northernmost third remaining under native control, and throughout the Roman period the province was subjected to hostile incursions from these northern tribes, as well as by sea-borne raiders from Ireland and north-west Germany. Until the third century AD Roman coins are at their most prolific on urban and military sites, with proportionally fewer being found on rural sites. This changed quite suddenly in the later part of the third century, owing partly to a much increased output of coinage, but also possibly to changes in the Roman military structure, which may have seen troops deployed away from military camps and perhaps acting as a militia spread throughout the countryside. It may be that town-based magnates were moving to their country 'villa' estates and taking military protection with them, but, whatever the reason, Roman coins from the mid-third century onwards are very common site finds on even the smallest of rural sites.

The end of Roman Britain is conventionally given as AD 410, although recent scholarship questions the precision of this. Whatever the exact date, the last Roman coins to reach Britain in the capacity of a regular currency terminate with issues of AD 402. Some of these occur in quite worn condition and seem to confirm archaeological and historical accounts suggesting that, at least in parts of Britain, a monetary economy continued well into the second quarter of the fifth century. But with the exit of the imperial army the British economy was radically changed and coinage ceased to be a part of everyday life, until reintroduced some two centuries later.

GOLD COINS

Aureus of Trajan (AD 98–117), 19 mm.

Solidus of Honorius (AD 393–423), 21 mm.

SILVER *DENARII*

Brutus (43 BC), 19 mm.

Tiberius (AD 14–37), 19 mm.

Tiberius – silver-plated contemporary copy, 19 mm.

Nero (AD 54–68), 19 mm.

Trajan (AD 98–117), 19 mm.

Hadrian (AD 117–38), 19 mm.

Antoninus Pius (AD 138–61), 19 mm.

Septimius Severus (AD 193–211), 18 mm.

SILVER *DENARII*

Septimius Severus (AD 193–211), cast white metal contemporary copy, 18 mm.

Antoninus 'Caracalla' (AD 198–217), 19 mm.

Severus Alexander (AD 222–35), 19 mm.

Julia Mamaea (died AD 235), 19 mm.

SILVER *ARGENTEUS*

Carausius (AD 287–93), 19 mm.

SILVER AND BASE-SILVER RADIATES

Gordian III (AD 238–44), 23 mm.

Valerian I (AD 253–68), 22 mm.

Postumus (AD 259–68), 22 mm.

SILVER '*SILIQUAE*'

Constantius II (AD 337–61), 18 mm.

Valens (AD 364–78), 17 mm.

Gratian (AD 378–83), 16 mm.

Arcadius (AD 383–408), 17 mm.

COPPER-ALLOY *SESTERTII*

Antoninus Pius (AD 138–61), 31 mm.

Faustina Senior (died AD 141), 32 mm.

Severus Alexander (AD 222–35), 30 mm.

COPPER-ALLOY *DUPONDII*

Trajan (AD 98–117), 28 mm.

Antoninus Pius (AD 138–61), 27 mm.

COPPER-ALLOY *ASSES*

Claudius (AD 43–54), 29 mm.
(Most found are irregular issues.)

Domitian (AD 81–96), 27 mm.

Hadrian (AD 117–38), 27 mm.

Antoninus Pius (AD 138–61), 26 mm.

COPPER-ALLOY RADIATES

Gallienus (AD 260–68), 19 mm.

Claudius II (AD 268–70), 19 mm.

Victorinus (AD 268–70), 19 mm.

Tetricus I (AD 270–73), 19 mm.

Tetricus II (AD 270–73), 18 mm.

Aurelian (AD 270–75), 20 mm.

Contemporary copy of Claudius II
(AD 270–87), 14 mm.

Contemporary copy of a radiate (AD 270–87),
12 mm.

Carausius (AD 287–93), 22 mm.

Allectus (AD 293–96), 18 mm.

COPPER-ALLOY *NUMMI* (AD 294–330)

Genius, Maximianus, 27 mm.

Sol, Constantine I, 19 mm.

Victories holding shield, Constantine I, 19 mm.

Captives below standard, Constantine II, 19 mm.

Altar, Constantine II, 19 mm.

Vota in wreath, Constantine I, 19 mm.

Sarmatia, Constantine I, 19 mm.

Gateway, Crispus I, 18 mm.

COPPER-ALLOY *NUMMI* (AD 330–48)

Victory on prow, 19 mm.

Wolf and Twins, 19 mm.

COPPER-ALLOY *NUMMI* (AD 330–48)

Two soldiers and two standards,
Constantine I, 19 mm.

Two soldiers and one standard,
Constantine I, 16 mm.

Contemporary copy, wolf and twins, 14 mm.

Pax, Helena, 15 mm.

Pietas, Theodora, 15 mm.

Two victories, Constans, 15 mm.

COPPER-ALLOY *NUMMI* (AD 348–64)

Soldier dragging captive from hut, Constans, 21 mm.

Phoenix, Constans, 17 mm.

Chi-rho, Magnentius, 25 mm.

Emperor and standard, Magnentius, 21 mm.
(Most found are irregular issues.)

COPPER-ALLOY *NUMMI* (AD 348–64)

Two victories, Magnentius, 20 mm.

Fallen horseman, Constantius II, 19 mm.

Fallen horseman, contemporary copy, 12 mm.

COPPER-ALLOY *NUMMI* (AD 364–78)

Emperor dragging captive,
Valentinian I, 18 mm.

Emperor with standard, Gratian
(only struck by this emperor
at Arles), 18 mm.

Victory with wreath,
Valentinian I, 18 mm.

COPPER-ALLOY *NUMMI* (AD 378–402)

Vota in wreath, Gratian, 14 mm.

Gateway, Magnus Maximus, 14 mm.

Victory with wreath, Theodosius I, 13mm.

Victory dragging captive, Arcadius, 14 mm.

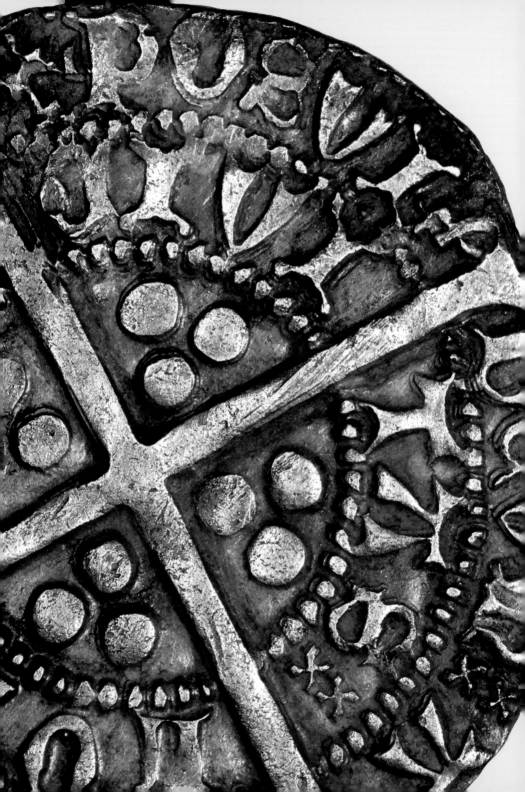

MEDIEVAL COINS

THE MEDIEVAL PERIOD is defined as the time between the fall of the Western Roman Empire and the Renaissance. For the purpose of classifying British coinage it is convenient to terminate the period with the accession of King Henry VII of England and King James IV of Scotland, in 1485 and 1488 respectively. The beginning of the period is popularly termed 'the Dark Ages'. This is not because they were a time of great misfortune for the native population, although they probably were, but because there is very little written evidence for what happened in Britain after the collapse of the centralised Roman administration.

Throughout the Roman period, the Empire had been subjected to incursions from tribes beyond the frontiers. Hibernian, Caledonian and Germanic raiders attacked the Roman province of Britain, and Franks, Goths and other eastern European tribes attacked Gaul and Italy. By the fifth century many of these invaders had established kingdoms of their own. In Gaul and Italy the newcomers adopted Roman ways and produced an imitative coinage, but in Britain they seem to have remained culturally aloof and no new coins were produced for the next two centuries. Britain, it seems, fragmented into a number of kingdoms, dominated in the east by Saxon overlords and in the west by native British ones. The early kingdoms may, at least to some extent, have followed Roman administrative boundaries and possibly earlier British tribal ones. By the time coins do reappear, the political face of Britain was one of fewer but larger kingdoms, which would eventually merge to leave just three, in the form of England, Wales and Scotland.

The first coins of Anglo-Saxon Britain were gold *tremisses* imported from Frankish Gaul, which were soon copied by English rulers. These are conventionally referred to as 'thrymsas'. Rapid debasement of the Frankish gold coinage followed, resulting in a large coinage of silver deniers; some were struck in the Low Countries and seem to have circulated freely both sides of the North Sea. These, as well as English issues, are known as 'sceattas' to English numismatists. By the beginning of the eighth century a complex

Opposite:
The reverse of a
groat of Henry V
(1413–22), 25 mm.

31

Gold *tremissis* struck in France (late sixth–seventh century), found in eastern England, 11 mm.

English 'sceat' coinage was being produced, which in the kingdom of Northumbria debased into copper-alloy issues, known as 'stycas'. Later in the eighth century the Franks introduced a new, broad-flan denier, and this was taken up by the English kings, the coins now being referred to as pennies. The silver penny was to remain the highest denomination coin in production until the thirteenth century, save for a few specially struck and extremely rare gold pieces.

In Wales, there was no native coinage save for a single and very rare issue of Howel Dda struck in the mid-tenth century, with English coins circulating instead. No coins were produced by the Scots until David I took Carlisle in 1136, when they commenced striking coins based on the English pattern.

By the time of the Norman Conquest, there were over seventy towns in England with mints engaged in the striking of coins. Although the largest output was from London, York and other major provincial cities, many smaller mints were also involved. Later Saxon and Norman coins carry the names of both the mint town and also that of the moneyer, who was an official tasked with overseeing the production of the coins. By the thirteenth century the number of English mints had reduced considerably and from the reign of Edward I these were confined to four cities, the names of the moneyers no longer being included. In Scotland, Alexander III produced a new issue of pence to coincide with the English re-coinage of 1279, likewise without moneyers' names, but initially struck at some eighteen different mint towns.

Although the penny remained the only denomination, it had become the practice from the later Saxon period to create small change by physically cutting the coins in half ('halfpennies') or into quarters ('fourthlings', or 'farthings'). This was further facilitated from the late twelfth century by the provision of a voided cross on the reverse. Although a few round fractions were occasionally struck, these are very rare and the cut coinage remained the norm until the reign of Edward I, when a new coinage of pennies, round halfpennies and round farthings was introduced. A new four-penny piece known as the groat was also struck, although this was initially short-lived.

In the mid-fourteenth century, Edward III of England reintroduced the groat and a new halfgroat, as well as a gold coinage of a noble, valued at 6 shillings and 8 pence, with fractions of a half and quarter noble. This coinage structure remained unchanged until Edward IV introduced a new gold coin valued at 10 shillings, called the ryal, but this was soon replaced by a new 6s 8d coin called the angel. 6s 8d had become established as a standard professional fee and the denomination was much missed. In Scotland, David II also introduced a noble and groat but the gold coinage was short-lived and it was not until *c.* 1390, during the reign of Robert III, that a new gold coinage was produced in the form of a lion of 5 shillings and a half-lion of 2s 6d. Further new gold denominations, the rider and unicorn, were introduced by James III. Unlike that of England, the Scottish coinage underwent debasement during the reign of James II, and under James III a base-silver plack was introduced, along with copper-alloy farthings.

Throughout the medieval period, coins from other parts of Europe were also used in Britain. At a time when a coin's value related to its bullion content, it was the metal, not the notional value, that counted. During the Viking era silver coins were initially regarded only as bullion, and in this context even coins from the Islamic world were traded as far as Britain and occasionally turn up as site finds. During the thirteenth and fourteenth centuries, the purity of English silver coins was such that English issues were widely imitated in the Low Countries and many of these 'sterling imitations' found their way to Britain, where, being of lesser purity, they were proscribed. Scottish coins circulated widely in England and English coins in Scotland, but only at times when the metal content was on parity. Ireland was invaded by the English in the twelfth century, and coins struck for use there turn up in England on occasion, as do issues struck for the English enclaves of Aquitaine and Poitou in France.

Medieval coins tend to occur as site finds in a less concentrated way than with Iron Age and Roman coins, which often cluster on discrete sites. Early medieval coins, the so-called 'sceats', do occasionally cluster and may relate to occupation sites or trading centres but later Saxon and Norman coins are very rare as site finds and may not have circulated in the same way. It is only with the new 'short cross' coinage issues from 1180 that coins become more prolific as field finds, owing in part to the increased number of coins being produced but also perhaps to demographic and other cultural changes. The commonest types of medieval coin to be found by archaeologists and metal-detector users are pennies and fractions from the late twelfth century onwards. Owing no doubt to the intrinsic value of the coins, groats and halfgroats are less common, with gold coins being very rare indeed. Most coin finds, we might assume, represent accidental losses, but some may reflect the practices of earlier times and be votive offerings. Occasionally a coin is found that has been carefully folded in two; these, we learn from contemporary writings, were deliberate ritual acts and the coins themselves may have been intentionally deposited in a location deemed auspicious at the time.

A selection of medieval coins recovered from an English field – all single losses (largest coin 19 mm).

GOLD COINS

'Thrymsa' (c. 600–700), 11 mm.

Henry VI (1413–22),
quarter-noble, 20 mm.

Edward IV (1461–83),
angel, 27 mm.

ANGLO-SAXON 'SCEATS' (c. 680–850, c. 12 mm)

Series 'A'.

Series 'B'.

Series 'E'.

Series 'F'.

Series 'M'.

Series 'S'.

Secondary phase imitation.

Northumbrian 'styca'.

ENGLISH PENNIES, EIGHTH TO TWELFTH CENTURIES (c. 18–20 mm)

Burgred (852–74).

Eadgar (959–75).

Edward the Confessor (1042–66).

William II (1087–1100).

Henry I (1100–35).

Stephen (1135–54).

Henry II (1154–89), 'Tealby' type.

John (1199–1216), 'short cross' type.

Henry III (1247–72), 'long cross' type.

Cut halfpenny and cut farthing.

ENGLISH COINS, THIRTEENTH TO FIFTEENTH CENTURIES

GROATS (c. 25 mm)

Edward III (1327–77).

Henry V (1413–22)

Edward IV (1461–83).

HALFGROATS (c. 21 mm)

Edward III (1327–77).

Richard II (1377–99).

Henry V (1413–22).

Henry VI (1422–61).

PENNIES (c. 19 mm)

Edward I (1272–1307).

Richard II (1377–99).

Henry IV (1399–1413).

Henry V (1413–22).

Edward IV (1461–83).

Richard III (1483–85).

HALFPENNIES (c. 13–15 mm)

Edward II (1307–27).   Edward III (1327–77).   Henry VI (1422–7).

FARTHINGS (c. 11 mm)

Edward I (1279–1307).   Edward II (1307–27).   Edward III (1327–77).

SCOTTISH MEDIEVAL COINS

William I (1165–1214), penny, 17 mm.

Alexander III (1249–86), penny, 19 mm.

David II (1329–71), groat, 27 mm.

Robert II (1371–90), halfgroat, 19 mm.

Robert III (1390–1406), halfgroat, 19 mm.

Robert III (1390–1406), penny, 18 mm.

James I (1406–37), groat, 24 mm.

James III (1460–88), copper-alloy penny, 18 mm.

COINS FROM OTHER COUNTRIES FOUND IN BRITAIN

France, Aquitaine, Prince Edward (1253–73),
denier au lion, 19 mm.

France, Charles IV (1322–28),
maille blanche, 23 mm.

Ireland, Edward I (1272–1307), penny, 19 mm.

Ireland, Edward IV (1461–83), penny, 14 mm.

Italy, Venice, Tomaso Mocenigo (1413–23),
soldino, 15 mm.

Low Countries (thirteenth century),
voided long-cross copy, 18 mm.

Low Countries, Holland, Floris V (1256–96),
denier, 14 mm.

Low Countries, Hainaut, John de Avesnes
(1290–95), sterling, 20 mm.

Low Countries, Brabant, Charles the Bold
(1467–77), double petard, 27 mm.

Portugal, Alfonso V (1438–81),
chinfrao, 18 mm.

POST-MEDIEVAL COINS

THE MEDIEVAL PERIOD, covered in the previous chapter, lasted some nine hundred years and yet, in terms of changes to the coinage, there were few innovations. Coins throughout the Middle Ages were often of very standardised and repetitive design, and all were produced with the same ancient technology, by manually placing a blank between two dies and striking them together with a hammer. In the five hundred or so years that have followed, the coinage has undergone many radical changes with many new denominations being introduced and some abandoned, and decimalisation has replaced the old monetary system. Stylistically, the medieval stereotyped portraiture was replaced in the fifteenth century by new and realistic Renaissance styles, firstly with the issues of James III of Scotland, and shortly after with those of Henry VII of England. The greatest change of all, however, was the move from manual to mechanised striking. The first attempt at mechanisation in Britain came during the reign of England's Elizabeth I, when a horse-powered screw press was used, but the method proved unpopular. A further century was to pass before another type of screw press came into use, which this time completely supplanted hammered coins, although they continued to circulate until demonetised in the reign of William III.

At the time of the ascension to the English throne of James VI of Scotland as James I of England, the coins issued in the two countries were quite different, but after 1603 conformed more closely, although with different values at point of issue but interchangeable at agreed rates either side of the border. Unlike England, Scotland had an established copper-alloy coinage, and this continued independently from the token farthings introduced in England under royal licence by King James. Another symbolic difference was the orientation of the portraiture. From the reign of King James it became the custom to alternate between right-facing and left-facing busts with each successive monarch. This was maintained as opposite-facing in the two countries, until the Act of Union in 1707 ended any difference in coin design, and the same issues prevailed throughout Britain.

Opposite:
The reverse of
an Elizabeth II
two-pence coin.

A gold sovereign of Elizabeth I. Such coins were struck in large numbers but never occur as site finds (42 mm).

It is no coincidence that the range of coin denominations increased with the expansion of British overseas interests. The Scots established a colony in Nova Scotia and the English did likewise in New England, as well as the East Indies. More trade meant more commodities in the home market which needed money to pay for them, and there is a noticeable increase both in the quantity of coin finds from the sixteenth century and the higher value of the denominations being used and subsequently lost. Although it is still rare to find gold coins or high-value silver, Elizabethan sixpences are surprisingly prolific, as are the lesser denominations such as threepences, halfgroats and pennies. Shillings remain a rare find until the reign of James I, but during his reign seem to have circulated more widely. During the Stuart period several attempts were made to alleviate the demand for small change. In Scotland copper-alloy 'turners' or twopences were in widespread use whilst in England farthings were issued by individuals operating with licences from the king. These English farthings were widely forged and so in the reign of Charles I a new kind of token farthing was introduced, known as the 'rose' farthing after the reverse design and which contained a copper insert. These were generally successful and are extremely common field finds in southern England.

If coin use and loss were prolific in the early post-medieval period, things changed drastically with the introduction of a new milled coinage in the reign of Charles II. He introduced a gold, silver and copper coinage that was to remain the basis for the British system for over three centuries, and yet very few coins in precious metal found their way into the ground, other than very low denominations such as silver pennies and twopences. However, the copper farthings struck from 1672 are probably nearly as common as the earlier 'rose' farthings. Charles II also introduced a coinage of tin farthings, which very occasionally turn up. Finds of James II are rare but those of his successor, William of Orange, occur mainly as sixpences, many of which are extremely worn and bent in an 's' shape, apparently as love tokens. Their frequency and wear suggest that the practice and their loss may date from a century or more later. By the early eighteenth century, the value of silver had risen to a point where a silver coin was worth more as scrap than it was as a coin of its face value. Not surprisingly coins disappeared almost as soon as they were issued, leading to a chronic shortage of coins and a virtually zero loss rate –

silver coins from the reigns of Queen Anne to George II are very seldom found as site finds and it was only with the new coinage of George III, introduced in 1816, that some coins such as shillings and sixpences occur in any numbers. Just occasionally higher-value coins of the preceding monarchs do occur, but they are usually very worn and may represent coins that were hoarded during the time of high bullion prices, and which were returned to circulation many decades later.

As far as field finds of the late seventeenth to early nineteenth centuries go, most are copper halfpennies and farthings, and even they are not as common as earlier hammered issues. Part of this may be down to the small and light hammered coins being more easily lost, but also perhaps due to changes in the agricultural system. The enclosure acts of the eighteenth and nineteenth centuries may have changed the way that the new fields were manured, and the importation of domestic waste for this purpose may have given way to other sources of fertiliser. Certainly by the mid-nineteenth century nitrate-based fertilisers were becoming more commonplace, which would of course be devoid of any domestically lost coins and other artefacts. Field finds of early nineteenth-century coinage in any metal are scarce, and it is only from late in the reign of Queen Victoria that single-coin finds occur with any regularity.

One problem that has dogged coinage from the earliest times is that of forgery, and the post-medieval period is no exception. Despite it being a capital offence punishable by hanging, drawing and quartering for men and being burned at the stake for women, forgery was rife. Coins from Tudor and Stuart times turn up that are base metal with a silver or tin coating and by the eighteenth and nineteenth centuries highly competent die-struck copies of coins were being produced, sometimes in plated base metal but sometimes silver-gilt. It is thought that these may have been the products of button makers, who not only had the skills of die engraving but also the machinery capable of producing highly competent forgeries. The problem persists to this day, with many pound coins in circulation being cast or struck forgeries.

As in earlier times, some coins from other parts of Europe circulated alongside British ones, usually without official sanction. The Venetian *soldini* of the fifteenth century reappeared some hundred years later in a slightly different format and these circulated as small change despite official attempts to outlaw them. French gold coins were widely used in Tudor England and some were even declared legal tender. Gold coins from Spain and Portugal were also used, although they only occasionally occur as recovered losses. Smaller denominations from all these countries do, however, turn up from time to time.

A silver-gilt contemporary forgery of a George III sovereign, 21 mm.

43

ENGLISH COINS

HENRY VII (1485–1509)

Penny, 16 mm.

Halfgroat, 19 mm.

Halfpenny, 12 mm.

HENRY VIII (1509–47)

Angel, 28 mm.

Groat, profile bust, 24 mm.

Halfgroat, profile bust, 18 mm.

Halfgroat, three-quarters bust, 18 mm.

Penny, 16 mm.

Halfpenny, 9 mm.

Farthing, 9 mm.

EDWARD VI (1547–53)

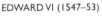

Shilling, 32 mm.

Sixpence, 27 mm.

MARY/PHILIP & MARY (1553–58)

Shilling, 26 mm.   Groat, 22 mm.

Penny, 16 mm.

ELIZABETH I (1558–1603)

Sixpence, 25 mm.   Groat, 22 mm.

Threepence, 18 mm.   Halfgroat, 16 mm.

Penny, 14 mm.   Threefarthings, 13 mm.   Halfpenny, 9 mm.

JAMES I (1603–25)

Gold halfcrown, 18 mm.

Shilling, 30 mm.

Sixpence, 26 mm.

Halfgroat, 16 mm.

Penny, 'portrait' type, 13 mm.

Penny, 'rose' type, 13 mm.

Farthing, 'Harrington' type, 15 mm.

Farthing, 'Lennox' type, 15 mm.

CHARLES I, 1625–49

Halfcrown, 35 mm.

CHARLES I, 1625–49

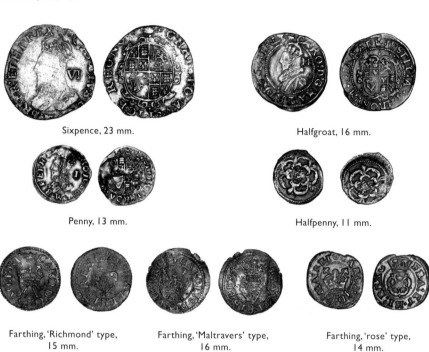

Sixpence, 23 mm.

Halfgroat, 16 mm.

Penny, 13 mm.

Halfpenny, 11 mm.

Farthing, 'Richmond' type,
15 mm.

Farthing, 'Maltravers' type,
16 mm.

Farthing, 'rose' type,
14 mm.

THE COMMONWEALTH, 1649–60

Halfgroat, 16 mm.

Penny, 13 mm.

CHARLES II, 1660–85

Guinea, 24 mm.

Farthing, 22 mm.

WILLIAM & MARY, 1688–94

Halfpenny, 29 mm.

Tin farthing, 22 mm.

WILLIAM III, 1694–1702

Sixpence, 21 mm.

Twopence, 14 mm.

ANNE, 1702–14

Shilling, 25 mm.

GEORGE I, 1714–27

Shilling, 25 mm.

Farthing, 23 mm.

GEORGE II, 1727–60

Halfpenny, 28 mm.

GEORGE III, 1760–1820

Third-guinea, 17 mm.

Sixpence, 19 mm.

Penny, 2nd issue
'cartwheel' type, 35 mm.

Halfpenny, 1st issue, 29 mm.

Halfpenny, 4th issue, 28 mm.

Farthing, 3rd issue, 22 mm.

GEORGE IV, 1820–30

Farthing, 20 mm.

WILLIAM IV, 1830–37

Shilling, 23 mm.

VICTORIA, 1837–1901

Sovereign, 21 mm.

Sixpence, 19 mm.

Penny, 30 mm.

Halfpenny, 25 mm.

Farthing, copper issue, 21 mm.

Farthing, bronze issue, 20 mm.

EDWARD VII, 1901–10

Halfpenny, 25 mm.

Farthing, 20 mm.

GEORGE V, 1910–36

Shilling, 23 mm.

Penny, 30 mm.

Farthing, 20 mm.

GEORGE VI, 1936–52

Shilling, 23 mm.

Threepence, 21 mm.

Halfpenny, 25 mm.

ELIZABETH II, 1952–

Pound, 22 mm.

Sixpence, 19 mm.

Halfpenny, 25 mm.

SCOTTISH COINS

Francis & Mary (1558–60), lion, 15 mm.

James VI (1567–1625), plack, 20 mm.

James VI, hardhead, 19 mm.

James VI, turner, 18 mm.

Charles I (1625–49), twenty pence, 16 mm.

Charles I, turner, 16 mm.

Charles II (1660–85), merk, 26 mm.

Charles II, turner, 19 mm.

William & Mary (1689–94), turner, 19 mm.

William II / III (1694–1702), bawbee, 25 mm.

COINS FROM OTHER COUNTRIES FOUND IN BRITAIN

FRANCE

Napoleon III (1852–70),
10 centimes, 30 mm.

IRELAND

James II, 'gunmoney' shilling, 25 mm.

George II, halfpenny, 29 mm.

ITALY

Venice, Agostini Barbarigo
(1486–1502), *soldino*, 12 mm.

LOW COUNTRIES

Holland (1766), duit, 21 mm.

Liège, Maximillian de Daviere
(1650–88), liard, 23 mm.

Overijssel (1619), 2 stuivers, 20 mm.

Zeeland (1741), duit, 21 mm.

TOKENS, COUNTERS AND MEDALS

S O FAR IN THIS BOOK we have examined the types of coins commonly found in the soil of Britain, but there are in addition a whole range of tokens and counters that turn up on a regular basis. The difference in definition is that a coin is something issued with state authority, whereas a token is something with a notional value, but which does not have official backing or intrinsic value. Tokens were often issued by traders as a means of supplying small change, which was often inadequate for the needs of the poorer classes. Tokens might be given in change and could be redeemed for coins of the realm, or they might be given as a receipt for a task performed and be redeemed for money or goods. Until recent times the hop growers of Kent gave a token to their pickers for every bag of hops filled, and these could be redeemed for a cash payment at the end of the day. Although tokens are quite common, we do not really know that much about how the early ones were used, nor can we even date them very closely. They seem to have become popular from around the thirteenth century, when they were mostly made of lead and a tentative chronology has been established, with some later lead, tokens actually bearing eighteenth-century dates, although most undated ones are thought to be earlier. In the mid-seventeenth century the lack of small change led many traders to produce machine-made tokens, mainly farthings and halfpennies, and between 1648 and 1672 many hundreds of traders and a few municipalities throughout Britain had tokens struck. A similar situation reoccurred in the eighteenth century, when local traders again had tokens struck, this time often having their names impressed into the edge of the tokens. There is little to suggest that seventeenth-century tokens inspired contemporary collecting interest, but eighteenth-century ones certainly did, and whole series of tokens were struck for the collector market more than for use as tokens. Tokens also afforded forgers a unique opportunity, as the penalties for forging tokens were nothing like as severe as those for forging coins of the realm. Some were struck with the general appearance of current copper coins, but with entirely fictitious legends, thus avoiding any obvious accusation of forgery. No doubt the largely illiterate

Opposite:
Detail of a
fourteenth- to
fifteenth-century
French jeton,
26 mm.

population would have struggled to tell the difference, which is why they were produced. Such pieces are known as 'evasions'. After this time the use of tokens as general currency ceased, but tokens continue to be used to this day, now mainly with gaming machines.

Perhaps more frequently found than tokens are reckoning counters, or 'jetons' as they are also known. Like tokens, these had their origins in the Middle Ages, and were used on a chequer board to perform calculations. Before the advent of Arabic numerals, it was not possible to calculate with Roman numerals in the same way, and so abacuses were widely employed to do mathematical reckoning. The chequer board was simply a two-dimensional version of the abacus, upon which counters were moved instead of beads on rods. It is from this early form of accounting that we get our Chancellor of the Exchequer. The counters themselves were die-struck and were modelled on coins of the time. Some early English jetons employed the same dies as were used to strike the sterling silver coinage, so clearly their production was under official supervision. Most of the medieval jetons found in Britain were struck in France, where their production was a thriving industry. Some have many design similarities with gold coins current at the time and one wonders if when new they may have occasionally been passed off as such, although no doubt any recipient would have been vigilant. By the end of the fifteenth century, the German city of Nuremberg began to supersede France in the production of jetons for export, although France continued to produce them in large numbers for the home market, where they came to be used as medallic tokens rather than as reckoning counters. The Nuremberg jetons become increasingly prolific in the late sixteenth and early seventeenth centuries, precisely the time when the use of Roman numerals was being replaced by Arabic ones for reckoning, and, as it was also a time of acute shortage of small change, it is highly probable that jetons were utilised as unofficial small change, something to which there are vague documentary references. The use of jetons died out at about the time regal copper farthings came in, which also hints at their monetary use.

Eighteenth-century 'evasion' with a fictitious legend, 29mm.

Medals, as commemorative pieces or military awards, also occasionally found their way into the ground, either through loss or simply by being discarded. Many thousands of commemorative medals have been produced over the years, and are often made from alloys of zinc, as well as gold, silver and copper-alloys. Until just after the First World War, British military medals usually had the name of the recipient around their edge, occasionally allowing recovered ones to be returned to relatives.

LEAD TOKENS

Pictorial type, c. thirteenth–fifteenth century,
17 mm.

Ecclesiastical 'boy bishop' type, sixteenth century,
19 mm.

Pictorial type, sixteenth–eighteenth century,
22 mm.

Sexfoil and initials, seventeenth–eighteenth century,
24 mm.

SEVENTEENTH-CENTURY TOKENS

Halfpenny, 20 mm.

Farthing, 16 mm.

EIGHTEENTH-CENTURY TOKENS

Halfpenny, 29 mm.

Halfpenny, 29 mm.

GAMING COUNTERS

Eighteenth-century 'guinea' counter, 22 mm.

Nineteenth-century political counter, 22 mm.

TWENTIETH-CENTURY TOKENS

Shop dividend check, 25 mm.

Gaming machine token, 20 mm.

JETONS, THIRTEENTH–FIFTEENTH CENTURY

English, king's head, 18 mm.

English, cross moline, 21 mm.

English, triangle, 21 mm.

English, heraldic, 21mm.

English and French, king under canopy, 22 mm.

French, shield of France, 27 mm.

French, dolphin, 25 mm.

French, crown, 25 mm.

JETONS, FIFTEENTH–SEVENTEENTH CENTURY

French, three lis, 26 mm.

French, Chatel Tournois, 25 mm.

French, IHS, 26 mm.

Nuremberg, French shield, 30 mm.

Nuremberg, ship, 26 mm.

Nuremberg, rose/orb type, 22 mm.

MEDALS

Victorian commemorative medal, 40 mm.

British 1914–18 War medal, 35 mm.

048-C0004
'Sceat'
ies 'A'

021-C0003
'Sceat'
as 'B'
r) 93

RECORDING COIN FINDS

W HEN ARCHAEOLOGISTS excavate a site, all small finds are meticulously plotted and will be entered on to a database, in order that when an excavation is finished and written up everything will have a context in relation to the whole site, to which future finds may be compared. When treasure hunting with metal detectors became popular in the 1970s archaeologists viewed this with alarm, as few metal-detector users had much understanding of archaeology, and seeking artefacts for personal collection or for sale went against all that archaeology stood for. This resulted in a stand-off for many years, until at last both sides came to appreciate that more could be gained through cooperation than by antagonism. Archaeologists came to realise that most of what metal-detector users found would never be recovered by conventional means, and that single scattered finds took on a context all of their own, in that they reflected general land use as much as activity in one spot. As a result a mechanism was developed whereby members of the general public could report archaeologically diagnostic finds and this information would be entered on to a database. At around the same time the archaic practice of Treasure Trove was replaced by new legislation, the Treasure Act, which has removed many of the anomalies that existed before.

The database that evolved is known as the Portable Antiquities Scheme (PAS), and it has a network of finds liaison officers covering most of Britain. Finds can be reported to them, and they will then enter the details on to the national PAS database. This database has already proved to be a valuable tool in reassessing many aspects of British history, and has been used as the basis for PhD research, as well as numerous other research-led projects. Many metal-detector users now recognise the value and mutual benefits that derive from cooperation, and a Code of Practice now exists that lays down recommended requirements for accurate recording and reporting. Anyone setting out to use a metal detector should familiarise themselves with both the Treasure Act and the Code of Practice, and discipline themselves to adhere to the requirements of these.

Opposite:
Excavated coins
after recording,
each individually
labelled and
archived in
storage trays.

Even when dealing with very worn or broken artefacts such as coins, although they will have little monetary value, they nonetheless have the same academic value as a find in perfect condition, and for this reason they need to be treated in exactly the same way. The most important piece of information is the precise find spot, and many metal-detector users now use GPS units to locate their finds to within 10 metres, which is perfectly adequate when dealing with finds loose in the ground. Finds are placed into plastic envelopes with write-on strips, and the find spot, in the form of a National Grid reference, is written on. This reference then stays with the find from then on. When dealing with coins, all finds should be properly cleaned and conserved, using basic guidelines available from the PAS. They will then be identified, measured and weighed and all this information entered on to the database along with the grid reference. A photograph containing a scale should also be taken, using a digital camera with a macro-lens. When all these data are finally uploaded to the PAS database, they add to the ever-growing corpus of information already recorded.

In addition to the PAS database, a number of other institutions or organisations have specialised listings to which PAS-derived data are normally passed. The Royal Numismatic Society publishes an annual list of newly found coin hoards in its journal, and the British Numismatic Society maintains a listing of new coin finds of particular interest in its own journal. The Fitzwilliam Museum in Cambridge is home to the Early Medieval Corpus, an index devoted to Anglo-Saxon and Norman period coin finds, and the Institute of Archaeology at Oxford houses the Celtic Coin Index, an archive of Iron Age coin finds, which has now been incorporated into the PAS system. All of these resources are available for consultation by the general public and provide additional research opportunities.

A computer and reference books – essential for the recording of coin finds.

FURTHER READING

CONTACTS

The Portable Antiquities Scheme, www.finds.org.uk
The British Numismatic Society, www.britnumsoc.org
The Royal Numismatic Society, www.royalnumismaticsociety.org

REFERENCE WORKS

Cottam, E.; de Jersey, P.; Rudd, C.; Sills, J. *Ancient British Coinage*. Chris Rudd, 2010.

Dickinson, M. *Seventeenth Century Tokens of the British Isles*. Seaby, 1986.

Duplessey, J. *Les Monnaies Françaises Royales*, volumes 1–2. Maison Platt and A.G. van der Dussen, 1988/9.

Elias, E.R.D. *The Anglo-Gallic Coinage*. Bourgey and Spink, 1984.

Grierson, P., and Blackburn, M. *Medieval European Coinage*. Cambridge University Press, 1986.

Hobbs, R. *British Iron Age Coins in the British Museum*. British Museum Press, 1996.

Krause, C.L., and Mishler, C. *Standard Catalogue of World Coins*. Krause Publications, 2012.

Mayhew, N.J. *Sterling Imitations of Edwardian Type*. Royal Numismatic Society, 1983.

Metcalf, M. *Thrymsas and Sceattas*, volumes 1–3. Royal Numismatic Society, 1993/4.

Mitchiner, M. *Jetons, Medalets and Tokens: The Medieval Period and Nuremberg*. Seaby, 1988.

North, J.J. *English Hammered Coinage*, volumes 1–2. Spink, 1991/4.

Sear, D. *Roman Coins and Their Values*, volumes 1–5. Spink, 2000–.

Spink. *Coins of Scotland, Ireland and the Islands: Pre-decimal Issues*. Spink, 2003.

Spink. *Coins of England and the United Kingdom*. Spink, 2012.

Van Arsdell, R. *Celtic Coinage of Britain*. Spink, 1989.

Various authors. *Roman Imperial Coinage (RIC)*. A multi-volume work written over many years and subject to ongoing revision and reprinting. Spink.

INDEX